SUMMARY OF
THE
PLANT
PARADOX:

THE HIDDEN DANGERS IN HEALTHY FOODS THAT CAUSE DISEASE AND WEIGHT GAIN

BY

STEVEN GUNDRY

Jessica Bridge

Table of Contents

EXECUTIVE SUMMARY

Steven Gundry, in this one book, challenges established beliefs that have formed the basis of many health programs and diets. "The Plant Paradox: The Hidden Dangers in 'Healthy Foods' That Cause Disease and Weight Gain", tells you that there's more to plant foods than what you've always been told. They are not the poster child for health and vitality as we've always thought. Actually, they can- *and have*- done so much harm to our bodies for the longest time.

Gundry is not hesitant to reveal facts that might be difficult to accept, like the fact that obesity and a bunch of other weight problems can be traced to consumption of certain plant foods. According to him, this is the reason a lot of folks are exercising and eating healthy, yet find it impossible to shed the weight.

In this book, Dr. Gundry traces the evolutionary history of plants, focusing on their composition as well as interactions with the human body. He instructs the reader on how to undo impairments that have been brought on by consuming the wrong plants. He also provides a list of plant foods fit for human consumption and how they should be eaten, as well as those unfit for consumption.

CHAPTER 1: THE WAR BETWEEN PLANTS AND ANIMALS

Key Takeaways

- *Plants/ Fruits can do both good, and harm*
- *Plants think!*
- *Lectins are more than just gluten*
- *You are what you eat!*

This chapter, in basic terms lays to bare what is required to achieve a slim stature, while maintaining a healthy, energetic lifestyle. A quick run through the last 400 million years sheds more light on a question that may be fast rising in your minds: Asking why knowing how plants work could influence you- to stating nothing of whether plants have goals of their own. As you journey through, you will realize that plants too, have a defense of their own, against plant predators, humans inclusive.

Undeniably, the consumption of certain plants is vital for good health. However, a paradox is found herein. These plants, essential as they may seem with regards to the provision of nutrients for survival, can also be the source of major health problems. A shocker that is, yeah? Well... here's a first. In the space of fifteen years, I have observed that the less fruits a patient consumed, the healthier the patient became. Not only that, the less seed- containing vegetables were consumed, the better the patients felt with regards to cholesterol levels and weight loss.

Living organisms are empowered to survive, and pass on these genetic factors to generations after them. It is important to note that although, as humans, we consider plants friends of ours, yet, they regard us foes. Thus, a battle ensues. Understanding that plants would consider humans; predators, the defense present in these plants serves as a discouraging factor to their consumption by humans. With this in mind, we understand therefore that although vegetables and fruits can help keep us alive and well, they equally have the tendency to do damage to our bodies and systems.

In what is known as the plant paradox program, a concept introduced and expatiated upon in this book, I largely examine how plants can hurt humans (sometimes) as opposed to the provision of nutrients and good health we are all accustomed to expect from its consumption (always).

A major example in this case is Gluten, a type of protein belonging to the lectin family. In recent times, gluten has been discovered to be harmful to some people, thus birthing the "gluten-free craze" that's taking over the medical and health scene. This concept, (plant paradox program) also presents the link between the different defensive chemicals present in plants and resultant effects such as diseases and weight gain.

The question as to whether plants have a goal or not is answered here. In direct words, like every other living thing, plants do not want to be eaten. In a bid to ensure a continuation of their species, they devised means to guard themselves against predators. Note carefully that this book does not stand against plant consumption; however, it does guide through the available plant options, teaching what should or should not be consumed as well as how and when such can be consumed.

Prior to the emergence of insects on the surface of the earth, plants had existed about 450 million years before. One can clearly imagine that it must have been a haven for plants, until those creatures came into existence. However, the intrusion into their space by creatures such as insects and primates sent plants into evolving various defense mechanisms to protect themselves and their seeds from predators. Such mechanisms include color blending, hostile feel, sticky substances and so on. Some defenses are much more indirect. Poisoning, paralyzing and confusing their predators are extraordinary defense mechanisms that plants have successfully employed in fending off predators.

The first set of predators that plants had to deal with were insects. This birthed the development of lectins to render insects paralyzed. And although lectins were developed to protect plants from insects, they nonetheless have similar effects on mammals. Having a huge number of cells as mammals, we may go on for years without experiencing any negative effects. Worse still, it might be happening to someone right now, who clearly does not even know it.

Often times, botanists refer to plant seeds as babies. Funnily enough, this is the real picture of things. After all, for continuity's sake, babies are born. In the plant world however, this is pretty tough as tons of seeds are produced, yet, only a few actually grow into becoming plants. There exist two basic categories of plant seeds. The first category consists of seeds enclosed in tough coatings, intended to be ingested by the predator. This is fashioned in such a way that the seeds can endure all the way through its predators' G.I. tract. The logic behind these type of seeds is this: the main plant is dependent on animals to consume the seeds before they go on to fall onto mother earth, with the intent of having these seeds, otherwise referred to as babies relocate elsewhere, in order to avoid competitions for basic survival elements such as sunlight, nutrients and moisture between the mother plant and the newly born plant. Thus, if the seed makes it out intact, it is accompanied with excreta from the animal, thereby increasing its chances of germination.

Armed with this hard casing, plants like these have no reasons to employ chemical defense strategies to protect their seeds. As a matter of fact, the plants employ various methods to attract the predator to themselves, encouraging the predator to eat their seeds. Such strategies include the use of color, where seeds take on the colors of fruits, communicating messages that their fruits are ready to be consumed, or not, via strategies which have been clearly devised by such plants. Here, the plants manufacture fructose, as opposed to glucose, with the goal of ensuring that the predator fails to get filled up, thereby creating a situation where more seeds are consumed, resulting in better chances of distributing the plants' "babies". On the flip side, increased consumption of fructose results in weight gain as a result of increased calories. And while this may be a win- win case for plants and animals (E.g., apes), it is not the same with humans. Why is this so? These fruits are no longer, unlike before, available only for a particular season of time. The availability of these fruits- all through the year makes you, not only sick, but overweight as well.

So far, we have learned that plants use colors to pass certain messages across. At this point, it is important to note that the color green means **STOP,** while the colors red, orange and yellow mean **GO.** This concept is not new to food vendors, as they have consistently employed this tactic in both food packaging and signage. With these colors in mind, we tend to classify red, orange or yellow colored fruits as ripe. Looks can be deceiving however, as this brings us back to the issue of seasons. Certain fruits are naturally available during particular seasons. However, slightly unripe fruits are sometimes picked, and a chemical compound known as Ethelyn oxide is added to such fruits, causing the fruit to change color, and appear ripe and ready for consumption. The harm here lies in that there still remains present a high level of lectin content, simply because the fruit failed to ripen naturally. By forcefully ripening the fruit and changing its color, the lectin content remains potent and dangerous to the human system. Hence, I recommend that only locally grown foodstuff be consumed, at key times in the course of the year.

There exists another category of seeds. These, referred to as "naked babies" do not have the tough, enclosed covering present in the former. The mother plant has no desire for these "babies" to be eaten. Here, plants choose a productive area to grow. The intention here is to have the "babies" fall in those particular spots, taking roots there. This way, the babies can sprout when the parent plants die off. The plant must consciously guard against its babies being carried off by insects and other predators. The seeds here contain chemicals that weaken, paralyze or cause predators to fall ill, thereby ensuring that the plants are left to grow.

These chemicals are contained in whole grains, which is a disclaimer to the popular misconception that whole grain is a nutritional awesomeness. Some other plants, most especially those which belong to the nightshade family, employ the use of tannins and alkaloids, which create bitter taste in the stems and leaves of plants such as tomatoes, peppers and some legumes. Also worthy of note is the fact that nightshades, including cooking preferences such as tomatoes are highly inflammatory.

So yes, we can conclude that plants do think, and perhaps, learn. Definitely, not in the same manner as humans. Yet, for the sake of survival and reproduction, they definitely are capable of intention. Recent research has also revealed that a plant knows when it's being eaten.

Lectins help plants greatly in defending themselves against predators, and equally play a pivotal role in hurting humans. In basic terms, lectins are huge volumes of proteins present in both plants and animals, a veritable tool employed by plants in defending themselves against animals. Contrary to common knowledge, there exist various other forms of lectin besides gluten.

Lectins, present in seeds, leaves and grains of most plants attach themselves to sugar molecules, cell surfaces, sialic acid, brain, nerve endings and bodily fluids present in the predator's body. This process of attachment causes toxic, or sometimes inflammatory reactions. Lectins are responsible for brain fogs. They also encourage the attachment of viruses and bacteria to their objects. This explains why some persons, those sensitive to lectins, are more easily affected by virus and bacterial infections than others.

In relation to weight, lectins have the capacity to stimulate weight gain. As a matter of fact, owing to small quantity of lectin in wheat, our ancestors gained and maintained weight. In the past, our ancestors devised means to deal with lectins. The reverse is the case now, as our generation has chosen to invent drugs and substances to reduce the pain that results from consuming these substances, just so that we can continue to eat them- not caring that they were intended to incite pain, destroy or even weaken us. A clear example of this is Nexium- a stomach acid reducer. To make matters worse, we do not stop at ourselves in this. Instead, we go on to feed animals; the same animals we would return to consume.

Lectins are a huge source of problems for humans. To begin with, we are not immune to these stuff. We are also incapable of breaking down these proteins. These result in all manners of health issues. But lectins are not limited to just beans and other legumes. The mere fact that cows, poultry and farm-raised seafood are being fed with grain- or soy based feed (which both have heavy lectin content), means these proteins find their way into the meat and milk gotten from these animals. It is therefore important to pay close attention to knowing how the food you eat was grown. Its impact on your health is much more direct than you can ever imagine.

Fortunately, in all of these, humans are not left without defense systems. The first line of defense available to humans is the mucus present in the nose, as well as the saliva present in the mouth. These two, when put together are referred to as mucopolysaccharides. Basically, the name indicates a combination of different sugars. Strictly, they capture lectins. Another defense strategy available to humans is the stomach acid. Third on this list is the bacteria present in the mouth and gut. Also, there is a layer of mucus created by certain cells through the intestines, acting as a barricade, using the sugars in the mucus to consume lectins. The brain is also a potent tool to battle lectins. Knowing the challenging state of some produce, they are best avoided or at least, their consumption rate reduced. Put together, a powerful system lies in place to guard against the harmful effects of lectins.

CHAPTER 2: LECTINS ON THE LOOSE

Key Takeaways

- *Lectins have been around for a long time.*
- *The most dangerous lectin? It's not Gluten!*
- *Wheat? Skip it!*

We have talked about lectins, and the effects they have on our health. Yet, a particular question still lingers. Why are we suddenly being affected by food containing lectins, after all, our ancestors have been eating these foods since time immemorial? Well, this is it! Lectins have been causing lots of damage for a long time. Humans and animals alike, through a process of trial and error, learned what we could, or could not eat. A while ago, however, the discovery of fire sent humans way ahead of all other creatures. To some extent, cooking reduces the potency of many lectins. This helped our ancestors to progress beautifully. Things however took a bad turn when the last Ice Age ended. Beans and grains became the order of the day; the weapon of the plant paradox. With these among us, lectins were launched into our midst, and we, thousands of years after, are still being caught unawares (just as we were those many years ago). These two, are the finest, yet the most horrible things that have happened to us.

There are two types of lectins- grazers and tree-dwellers. Humans are tree-dwellers. Gut bacteria is essential to the immune system as it trains it on what mixtures are harmful or harmless to the body. In eating patterns among humans, there are typically four interruptions that upset the stability that has always existed between plants and animals. These interruptions have forced a change in diet over time. Recently however, it has been discovered that lectins have a role to play in this, with diverse health problems pointing to the fact that the battle is not in our favor anymore.

The agricultural revolution birthed the consumption of grains and beans in most nations. Quickly, humans moved from eating tubers, animal fats and protein to consuming grains and beans. Ancient Egypt was able to feed its people with wheat. Over the years, however, research has revealed that lots of Egyptian mummies had serious health issues as most of them died overweight, and their arteries, congested. This interruption was closely followed by a mutation in cows in Northern Europe. Following this, another interruption ensued when Europeans got to

America, bringing food from their native land. Thus, the rest of the world became open to a whole new world of lectins, most of which were legumes, grains and other seeds. The last, and latest interruption is found in the release of lectins in processed foods and in genetically modified organisms. These sort of lectins are very foreign to the body, and the introduction of various drugs have destroyed the gut bacteria which would have helped process the lectins and serve as a trainer to the immune system. Our sudden sensitivity to lectins is hinged on our food options. In recent times, we have let go of most proper means of preparing and consuming food, and have settled for processed meals. Our diet has also undergone a major change, being heavily laced with lectin-containing food. The introduction of chemicals such as pesticides and herbicides also destroy the gut, and generally, the internal communication system.

I mentioned earlier that gluten is just one type of lectin, and the supposed danger that has received the most attention all this while. Food like wheat, barley, rye and oats all contain gluten. Consuming one or all of these foods, often considered healthy, can result in celiac disease. It is important to note that there are other lectins other than gluten, which are even more dangerous than gluten. Often times, products said to be devoid of gluten still contain other forms of lectins. This is the reason why my patients, even after they stopped the intake of barley, oats, rye and wheat still continued to have digestive or weight problems, simply because their gluten-free foods were not actually lectin-free.

For so long a time, Gluten has been considered the most dangerous of all lectins, particularly in wheat. The reverse is the case however. Gluten is not the bad guy. As a matter of fact, in Countries where gluten is the major source of protein, people live absolutely good and healthy lives. Research reveals however that Wheat Germ Agglutinin (WGA) is by far more dangerous than gluten. Whole grains have also been discovered to be high in lectin content. Thus, Asians who peel the hull off brown rice to make it white before eating it are really intelligent, as these hulls contain very high lectin.

Wheat is not healthy. Neither is glucosamine, which is naturally found in the body. Both can cause serious health issues. Thus, I advise that you simply avoid eating wheat as well as other lectin-containing food.

I noticed a particular pattern in my patients' health, and the gains they got from the diet program I placed them on. When I decided to switch from the use of the medical practices that treat disease symptoms to medical practices that allow the body heal itself, a lot of my first set of patients were overweight men who also had heart diseases. However, after running tests on their wives, it was evident that both husbands and wives were unhealthy, despite the fact that their wives were eating supposedly healthy meals. Most of the wives had arthritis, thyroiditis, among others, and often relieved their pains using different drugs. As a matter of fact, these women were placed on as many as seven different medications, yet they considered themselves healthy. Having noticed these, I changed their diets, husbands and wives alike. And in a short while, I steadily noticed the way their bodies naturally reversed the process of sicknesses, and healed itself.

Soon after, many women would come into my office seeking for help. At this point in time, many of them would be overweight or obese, with their health issues having been termed hormonal problems, anxiety or depression by their doctors. Others with diseases like rheumatoid arthritis, lupus and a host of others soon appeared, seeking for a way out. And once again, they got better, by simply following my food list.

CHAPTER 3: YOUR GUT UNDER ATTACK

Key Takeaways:

- *99% of our genes are non-human!*

- *As humans, we depend largely on microbes.*

- *Microbes are gotten from our mothers!*

- *It is possible to eradicate any autoimmune disease without having to use drugs*

Health issues are often caused by very minute things. In and within our bodies live lots of microbes. Often times, we are convinced that who we appear to be is who we really are. Yet, that is not true. We are, as a whole, what we appear to be along with these tons of microbes. As a matter of fact, a massive 99% of the genes present in us as humans are not even human. Don't freak out! The reality here is that initially, we tend to overlook the multiple-life forms with which we co-exist. However, we exist on this planet together with those microbes. Basically, we are not alone. They are present; in our skins and intestinal tracts.

The increase in the amount of microbes is referred to as the microbiome, although the term holobiome has been adopted by scientists as more fitting. It is important to note however that you house these microbes, and in return, they serve us as well. This may be quite difficult to believe, but as humans, we are largely dependent on microbes, and cannot even exist without them. These microbes are often at work, heavily, in our gastrointestinal (GI) tract, processing plant cell walls, hauling out energy and making it available to the body as fats.

And where do you get these microbes from? Your mother! Strange, but true. Upon leaving the birth channel, you become immunized with her set of microbes, which create your very first holobiome. This was very important for your growth and development, as it helped to train your immune system along with its cells. The holobiome consists of five pounds of organisms- bacteria, worms, protozoa, fungi, molds and viruses, all of which live in different parts of the body, playing a pivotal role in the entire body system. And although these cells are essential for proper functioning of the human body, other cells present in the body think that the former belong on your outside. It is crucial that these microbes remain on the outside, so as to prevent you from being contaminated. It is however a daunting task to have the holobiome in its place because it performs two entirely different roles.

There are certain things that should, or should not pass through the gut wall. Only minute distinct molecules of digested food should pass through the intestinal wall. Every food you consume must be broken down into molecules that the body can absorb.

Owing to changes in the stuff we consume, things do not work the way they should in the gut wall. Big proteins, without the help of WGA cannot get through the intestinal wall easily. Lectins however can tear the barriers that make up the intestinal mucosal border. With this opening, bigger molecules gain access into the body, where they also cause great damage. When these lectins make their way from the gut into the human body, the immune system considers this an attack on the body, signaling to the body to store fat and supplies for the supposed attack.

However, if lectins were really responsible for most of these health issues, how come other medical consultants have not mentioned it? The answer is simple! Except the eyes are open, one cannot see clearly. This is the exact issue with physicians and nutritionists. Owing to their ignorance on the effects of lectins, they believe that people can go on, eat lectins, including glutens, and remain healthy.

On a whole new note, you should know that it is possible to eradicate any autoimmune disease without having to use drugs. How? The solution lies in curing your leaky gut. According to research, all of these autoimmune diseases stem from the gut, and as such, can be cured by healing the gut. I am certain that these diseases are caused by a change in the good and bad microbes which live in the gut, mouth and skin, as well as a change in the penetrability of the gut wall, mouth and gums. This penetrability is enhanced by the consumption of NSAIDs, antibiotics, acid blocking drugs and a host of others, which alter the gut flora and its mucous layer, daily destroying the barrier wall of the intestines and thereby allowing lectins find their way in. These series of actions result in an attack by the immune system, a typical case of mistaken identity. This goes on and on, in a cause and effect sequence, and finally results in these diseases. However, they can be reversed. And to do this, one must stop consuming lectins.

How then can this be done? By having the good microbes back in your gut!

CHAPTER 4: KNOW THY ENEMY: THE SEVEN DEADLY DISRUPTORS

Key Takeaways:

- *Serious health challenges stem from minute things.*
- *Antibiotics are killer drugs!*
- *Bluelights- Summer never ends!*

There exist within the human body changes that are almost never noticed. Each and every of these huge things that have greatly changed us stem from very minute things which have very serious impact on our health. These, indirectly result in cravings for unhealthy foods or a need for more medications or medical measures. Slowly, we have come to depend on these medications and measures, as they appear to improve our health. The reverse is the case however, as they actually worsen our health conditions.

You might be surprised to find out that the very things you eat, use and drink everyday are capable of altering a lot of organisms that constitute who and what you are, yet, you have been told that these substances are good for you.

This chapter presents seven changes that have occurred over the years, and have strongly altered our health. The first is the introduction of broad-spectrum antibiotics into our world. Initially, these drugs were thought to be wonder-working drugs. With the ability to destroy loads of bacteria strains, they saved thousands of lives from different diseases. However, they allowed physicians destroy an infection without necessarily having to bother about what bacterium was a problem. Sadly, doctors still choose to use antibiotics, even when it is clear that the problem isn't bacteria, but a virus, and as such cannot be destroyed using antibiotics. Another shocking revelation is that while taking one or more of these antibiotics, we equally kill the microbes in our gut. These guts may not return for the next two years. Some never even return. Worse still, for every shot of antibiotic a child takes, the possibility of the child developing diabetes, asthma or obesity at a later period in life increases.

Nonsteroidal Anti-Inflammatory Drugs (NSAIDs) closely followed the introduction of antibiotics, serving as a replacement for aspirin which was widely known to destroy the lining of the stomach. NSAIDs are not safe however, as they equally destroy the mucosal barrier present in the colon, and small intestine, thereby allowing lectins have their way into the body.

Stomach acid blockers soon joined the list. At all costs, avoid them. Most of them do a good job of reducing the amount of stomach acid. Stomach acid however serves a very important function. Very few bacteria can tolerate stomach acid, thus, a lot of the bad bacteria you swallow are destroyed there. Here is the problem. In the absence of stomach acid to destroy the bad bacteria, they can overgrow, and go on to change the normal gut flora. Bad bacteria can also find their way into the small intestine, where they do not belong, and begin to create health challenges such as leaky gut or SIBO.

Artificial sweeteners? They change the gut holobiome, destroy the good bacteria and allow the bad ones overgrow.

Hormone disruptors? These are an array of chemicals present in preservatives, plastics, cosmetics and other diverse products along with dichlorodiphenyldichloroethylene (DDE), a metabolite of dichlorodiphenyltrichloroethane (DDT) and polychlorinated biphenyls (PCBs), which are constantly in a havoc game with our hormones.

Genetically modified foods and biocides are not left out in this. As good as these biocides may seem, their health implications are far more dangerous than we can imagine. Biocides and Genetically modified foods have led poisons into our systems through the food, produce and animals we eat.

Constant exposure to blue light is the last of these changes. For a long time, humans and other animals have constantly gotten food responding to changes in daylight, and particularly, the blue wavelength spectrum of daylight. When we have long days and short nights, our bodies are stirred to consume as much food as we possibly can, in readiness for winter. Also, when we have short days and long nights, our bodies are stirred to consume less food, and burn up all the fat we have gained during summer.

In recent times however, our lives have been dominated by the blue light, through the use of technological devices. The danger herein is that blue light subdues the production of melatonin, a hormone which helps in falling asleep. On the flip side, being sleep starved is connected to obesity. The blue light also rouses the hunger and awake hormones. And owing to the fact that our genetic make-up links blue light to daylight, our bodies are tricked into thinking we're in summer, allowing us eat and eat, in anticipation for winter, which never arrives. With this system in place, we perpetually live in summer, all year round.

CHAPTER FIVE: HOW THE MODERN DIET MAKES YOU FAT (AND SICK)

Key Takeaways

- *Disease issues and weight issues are related.*

- *The microbes in your gut help out in digestion.*

- *Lectins can mimic insulin and create serious problems.*

- *A good and effective diet should eliminate lectin-containing foods.*

Here, I give further evidence of how so many of my patients have lost weight significantly once they started the program. Our attention is drawn to how a simple change in diet as well as lifestyle could work wonders and benefit one's health. Fat in the body is seen as extra luggage and its presence in the body is owing to a wrong or inefficient diet. The Plant Paradox Program which I talked about in previous chapters is more concerned with the job of taking away what is irrelevant in your diet. At this point, I should emphasize that this chapter addresses disease issues and weight issues together because both of them are congruent with each other.

Another important thing I emphasize is that most people do not realize the job of our gut bugs in matters relating to weight. There are microbes that are responsible for weight loss while others help you add weight. There are also gut bugs that cause sickness thereby depriving you of a healthy weight. It is possible to be stuffing yourself with food, yet not adding any weight. This is because your gut bugs don't help out in digestion. As a result of this, you may be starved of the required calories and micronutrients. There are so many other factors that hinder effective digestion and availability of nutrients. However, I have noted that Celiac disease is just a shadow of these factors that cause malnutrition.

Furthermore, we see that being overweight or underweight means that your body is going through a war. We are taken back to the mid-1960s when public health began to experience a worrisome phase. This has accounted for 70.7% of today's American adults being overweight. In just two decades before today, the number of obese people among these adults has shot up from Twenty-nine percent to Thirty-eight percent. There are also much more cases of diabetes, heart disease, Parkinson's disease, to mention but a few. One in four persons is diagnosed with one or more autoimmune disease. Today's living conditions hasn't helped matters so much. Even with better feeding and more favorable working conditions, there is still the problem of low energy. Allergies are also on the rise. This is very concerning because nowadays even kids carry adrenaline shots to school. This is to be on the safe side in case they are exposed to peanuts. These kids can quickly inject themselves with their syringes. In light of all this, we have blamed the Western diet and the environment for our poor healthy living. However, these are not the major causes of our health condition.

We must go way back to twelve thousand years ago to truly understand what happened. At that time, the height of the average man was at six feet compared to a few thousand years later in 8000 BCE when that height was reduced to four feet ten inches. The agricultural revolution is responsible for this reduction. It is also responsible for introducing grains and legumes into our diet. Hence, from the mummified remains of the Egyptians to the skeletons of present day people (excluding those whose diet have very little lectin-containing foods), everyone suffers from arthritis. In addition to this, the average human's brain was 15 percent larger twelve thousand years ago than it is today.

Understanding what certain foods do to your body system and changing your eating habits will help you understand that it is not weight-loss programs you need. These programs end up becoming useless because they don't address the effects of what goes into your system. Although staying physically fit is good for your cardiovascular health, blood pressure and HDL cholesterol, these exercises don't help you lose weight. They rather make you hungry and become a burden to those who are overweight.

I take us back to when I addressed the scientific team of Metagenics, a major *nutriceutical* manufacturer, on the principles of my book, *Dr. Gundry's Diet Evolution*. As at that time, I was opposed to carbohydrates (sugars) because they caused all diseases. However, this did not apply to the South Pacific tribe of the Kitavans who pile up on 60 percent calories from carbohydrates and 30 percent from coconut oil. As a researcher, I had to revisit this phenomenon because the ills of carbohydrates did not just apply to Kitavans.

We have earlier seen that our ancestors opted for an agriculture-based diet ten thousand years ago. This allowed for their populations to remain in one place as they had foods that could be consumed all through the year. However, it is interesting to reason if their choice grains, beans, and milk was due to the fact that these foods are capable of optimizing fat storage per calorie more than any other foods. Hence, this is the best way to fatten up. Just as Ohio River Valley pigs were fattened with corn in the nineteenth century, so does eating corn fatten us up as humans. This is plausible because a pig has similar digestive and cardiovascular system with a human. However, we see another paradox here. As grains and nuts optimize fat in any calorie in order to aid reproduction and growth, so does it shorten our post-reproductive years.

We move on to see the lectin link to obesity and ill health. The pancreas secrete insulin into the bloodstream when sugar enters the bloodstream. This insulin gives way for any cell to transport glucose into fat cells, muscle cells and nerve cells. However, lectins tend to mimic insulin and attach themselves to the docking ports on cell walls instead. This could create some serious problems. The Wheat Germ

Agglutinin (WGA) has the properties of the hormone insulin. When WGA acts as insulin in a fat cell membrane, it continuously instructs the cell to keep on making fat from sugar. The WGA in a muscle cell blocks out the real insulin from coming in. This results in muscle wastage as we grow older. In the case of nerve cells and neurons, WGA refuses the entry of sugar hence making the brain demand more calories. In the long run, it kills brain cells and peripheral nerves, causes dementia, Parkinson's and peripheral neuropathy.

This chapter flows on to why we have so many diets. We see already established and popular diets such as low-carb, high-protein; low-carb, high-fat, high-protein; low-fat, high-carb. I've been privileged to treat a number of patients who followed these diet programs strictly. In spite of them being able to maintain their weight, they continued to have serious medical issues such as advancing coronary artery disease and autoimmune disease. What then is contained in these diet programs and how does it affect the followers? Ardent low-carb disciples will attest that this program works well only in the short term. Low-carb diets restrict carbohydrates and are high on protein content.

When grains and legumes are introduced back into the diet, along with it comes previously lost pounds. Some have suggested that what made our ancestors healthy was their diet which included buffalo and other large animals. This is known as the Paleo concept. However, this concept is flawed because our ancestral diet actually included tubers, berries, nuts, fish, lizards, snails, insects, and small rodents. This is so because such big kills of buffalo couldn't have occurred on a regular basis. It is important to note here that it is the elimination of lectin-containing foods that guarantee the success of a Paleo diet or a low-carb plan. This leads to another counter-argument to the Paleo concept which is that all our ancestors originated from Africa and were healthy because there was no chance of eating any lectin containing food there.

We look further to a ketogenic diet which, instead of substituting carbohydrates for protein, restricts the protein and gets its calories from certain fats instead. We define ketosis here which involves burning fat rather than glucose gotten from carbohydrates in order to get energy. It seems to be that most people in ketosis are on a ketogenic diet and that this is responsible for their weight loss. However, this is false because weight loss in ketosis is not as a result of the addition of fat, it is rather due to a significant removal of lectin-containing foods from the diet.

The weight loss in this diet plan is similar to that of the low-fat, whole-grain diets. In my experience, many of my patients on this diet plan had significant weight loss however they still had their coronary artery disease. The weight loss then is as a result of eliminating lectin-containing fats found in soy, peanut, cottonseed, sunflower, and canola. These foods which are common in our American diet are used to incite inflammation which is war declared against our coronary arteries. The reason the Chinese, Japanese, and Koreans, unlike the Americans have lower heart disease rate is because rice, their staple, has no WGA. This low heart disease rate is the same for Africans whose staples include sorghum, millet, and yams.

It is quite interesting to know that like elephants, which eat grains and hay, we have WGA and other lectins which are after our sugar molecule known as Neu5Ac. This lectin-binding sugar leads to a high rate of severe coronary artery disease due to the grains we consume. It is a different case in mammals whose sugar molecule, Neu5Gc is resistant to lectin. Hence, for us who have the lectin-binding sugar molecule, we are exposed to autoimmune diseases when we consume lectin-containing foods.

This is why fish eaters enjoy a better heart health than meat eaters. Neu5Gc, which is a foreign sugar molecule to our body is found in red meat. Because Neu5Gc looks very much like Neu5Ac, we develop an antibody from Neu5Gc when consumed and this antibody attaches itself to the lining of our own blood vessels. The result is that our own Neu5Ac is mistaken for Neu5Gc and puts our immune system on the offensive. I emphasize here that this is the case of a friendly fire. In essence, avoiding red meat is automatically avoiding autoimmune attacks that cause heart disease and cancer. The Kitavans, earlier mentioned, never experience strokes or heart attacks. This is because they carbohydrates they consume are resistant starches and almost free of calories. These resistant starches do not raise blood sugar or insulin levels.

In the 1970s, the eating menu of schoolchildren began to have a lot of pizza and chicken in it. These two foods are actually ticking lectin bombs waiting to explode. The result of this diet today is many obese kids. Hence, we must fight back to regain a healthy life.

CHAPTER SIX: REVAMP YOUR HABITS

Key Takeaways:

- *What you stop eating has more impact than what you start eating.*

- *Encourage the growth of your gut bugs and they will return the favor.*

- *Fruits can be as harmful as candy.*

- *Our body system has small protein needs.*

A journey through the four rules that govern the Plant Paradox Program guides us through this chapter. I advise you to commit these rules into memory. These four rules will guarantee success on the Plant Paradox Program. In the first rule, I emphasize that what you stop eating is more important to your health than what you start eating. This does not mean that you altogether stop eating. However, there are some foods that damage your gut. Your gut holobiome consists of all your genetic makeup. Speaking of your gut, rule number two requires that you pay good attention to the care and feeding of your gut bugs. This in return, will help your gut bugs work in favor of your system. Rule number one is foundation to this rule because if you keep feeding on sugar, refined carbs, and saturated fat, this will groom bad bugs in your gut. Stop encouraging their growth by feeding on junk food because these bad bugs thrive on them.

Rule number three brings fruits into the field of play. The rule is simple: fruits have the same harmful effects as candy. That bowl of fruit salad for breakfast turns out to be a bad idea. By fruit, I must emphasize that it consists of everything that has seeds. This is inclusive of a zucchini, a tomato, a bell pepper, an eggplant, and a pickle. Eating these is the same as eating an apple. They all send the same message to your brain which is that your body needs to store fat for the winter. Still on the fruit matter, there are some safe areas. Bananas, mangoes, and papayas which are still green are good for the body. However, eating the fructose in other fruits will cause injury and swelling to the kidneys. The only acceptable ripe fruit is the avocado which contains no trace of sugar. Rather, it contains good fat and soluble fiber to help you lose weight. Rule number four states that you are what the thing you are eating, ate. This means that you are automatically a consumer of an ear of corn and a pile of soybeans because that is what the producers of the meat, poultry, farm-raised fish, eggs, and dairy products you're eating, ate.

In this chapter, I have taken care not to mention how many calories you can consume a day. On the Plant Paradox Program, there won't be calorie counting or carb counting. We'll be watching out for our intake of animal protein instead. This program ensures that you give a fair share of calories to your gut buddies. Your gut buddies consume these calories and make them unavailable to you or even better change then into good fats that provide energy. As we go on, we'll see the foods we need to eat and those we need to avoid. Corn is one crop the average American cannot avoid. It is hugely present in processed foods. Fast food ingredients consists of cornstarch, cornmeal, corn syrup and the likes. Ninety-three percent of fast food burgers contain C-4 carbon. This shows that the burger came from animal whose diet was predominantly corn. This was the same for the diet of chickens used for chicken sandwiches. Scientists at the University of California-Berkeley discovered that carbon tested hair of typical Americans had Sixty-nine percent of corn. The corn fed to livestock in the United States is a genetically modified type called BT corn. It is high on insect-resistant lectin and is fed to livestock which is in turn consumed by us. This lectin is found in the breastmilk of American mothers.

Owing to this genetically modified corn, chickens develop osteopenia and osteoporosis. These are bone-deterioration diseases that are common only with postmenopausal women. Our livestock are housing antibiotic-resistant bacteria which results in several deadly disease outbreaks. Much more, we can find aflatoxins in chicken (eggs and flesh), pork, beef, and cow's milk. This toxic substance is harmful to animals and humans. It has led to genetic changes and cancer.

Going back to our second rule, as much as there can be bad bugs in one's gut there can also be good bugs. The good bugs protect and support your body system. And if you encourage their growth, soon enough all the bad bugs will be gone. Encourage the growth of the good bugs by eating the right things such as greens and vegetables. By doing this, the good bacteria demand for more of these that makes them happy. Much more, they help you manage your appetite and cravings. You do not have to suffer from the uncontrollable longing for junk food anymore.

These cravings which are more common with a high-protein, high-fat, low-carb diet disappear fish us the source of protein with greens and tubers offering sufficient resistant carbs. The Plant Paradox Program, unlike Paleo and ketogenic diets, takes away the presence of constant hunger by offering only the appropriate animal fats. The program has versions for everyone including vegetarians who don't eat meat, fish, or poultry as well as those who don't eat eggs or dairy products. We will learn that leaves provide us with a great deal of muscle-building protein just as it does for horses.

I'll introduce you to the basics of the Plant Paradox Program. They are in three phases. Phase one involves a three-day cleansing. This repairs the guts and encourages the growth of the good microbes while sending out the bad microbes. To prevent the bad microbes from returning, you must immediately move on to phase two. This phase is where the Plant Paradox Program kicks into full gear. It involves the removal of lectin-containing inclusive of whole-grain products. It eliminates all sugars and artificial sweeteners, industrial farm raised poultry and livestock. Your diet will now consist of leafy greens and vegetables, tubers and other resistant starch foods, omega-3 fats found in fish oil, and dairy products only from certain breeds of cows, sheep, goats and water buffalo. Phase three restricts animal protein to 2 to 4 ounces a day.

Consumption of the required amount of protein provides you with energy and helps in building muscle. However, the case with most Americans is that we consume much more protein than we need. This protein is predominantly from animals. The process of having to metabolize these animal protein leads to high blood sugar levels, obesity, and short life span. The big question then is how much protein we really need. You just have to divide your weight in pounds by 2.2 to get your weight in kilograms, then multiply the figure by 0.37 and this will reveal the amount of protein you need daily. Our needs for protein should be small because both our mucus and gut lining cells contain protein. We digest these proteins into our gut when we produce mucus or when our gut lining cells die and are replaced.

There is need for reconfiguration of your mental and physical elements. This is because they Plant Paradox Program, with its four rules, require you to cut out some foods which you have for long seen as healthy. These foods include whole grains, organic chicken, cow's milk yogurt, edamame, tofu amongst others. Some of my patients in the Plant Paradox Program have experienced significant changes by making sacrificial changes in their diet. However, there are excuses that are bound to keep you from moving forward with the program.

One of them is that you may feel that you shouldn't make any diet changes because you are already slim and fit. Another excuse is that you fear that you now have to understand a lot of metabolism and nutritional concepts. This is not true because I have non-English speaking patients who have had huge successes. The overall success of this program is actually narrowed down to following the rules on foods to eat and those to be avoided. A third excuse will be that you're too old to make significant changes in your eating and other habits. However, the elderly can also develop a strong willingness to make these sacrifices in their diet. It is never too late for anyone who is on this program to experience breakthroughs in their health.

CHAPTER SEVEN: PHASE 1 - KICK-START WITH A THREE-DAY CLEANSE

Key Takeaways

- *In this phase, your diet is mainly greens and vegetables.*

- *Items on your recipe include vegetables, protein, fats and oils, condiments and seasonings.*

- *A minimum of eight hours sleep is very much needed.*

- *Your choice of foods must be top quality.*

- *Start phase two on the morning of day four after the three-day cleanse.*

Phase one of the Plant Paradox Program is geared towards kicking out the bad bugs in your gut. These bacteria have been responsible for making you long for foods that are harmful to your gut. Preparation is made in this phase by embarking on a three day cleansing. At the end of these three days, the bad bugs will be replaced by good ones. These bugs are housed in your small intestine. It is of utmost importance that you immediately move into phase two once phase one is completed. This is to ensure that your efforts are not in vain and that the good bugs continue to hang around. The purpose of this three day cleanse in phase one is to seal off any reentry points for the evicted bad bugs. There are three components in the three day cleanse.

In the first component, you must adhere strictly to eating no dairy product, grains or pseudo-grains, fruit, sugar, seeds, eggs, soy, nightshade plants, roots, or tubers. Other foods to be taken out of your diet include corn, soy, canola, beef or meat from farm animals. Your new diet would rather consist of greens and vegetables as well as little amounts of fish. For vegans on the program, there's no need to fret as we also have a plan for your own tailored diet.

These following recipe rules for component one must be strictly followed. For vegetables, it is safe to stay with the cabbage family which includes Bok choy, broccoli, Brussels sprouts, and kale. Not forgetting greens like spinach, Swiss chard, watercress and all kinds of lettuce. Other vegetables which have a go-ahead are artichokes, asparagus, celery, fennel, radishes, parsley, basil and all kinds of onions. For patients with irritable bowel syndrome (IBS), SIBO, diarrhea or any other gut issue, raw vegetables should be limited.

We move on to the protein part of the recipe. You are to eat no more than 8 ounces of wild caught fish or pastured chicken daily. These come in the size of two 4-ounce portions. Hass avocados are the best source of fats and oils. Any kind of olive also has a green light. Recommended oils include avocado oil, coconut oil, macadamia nut oil, sesame seed oil, walnut oil, extra-virgin olive oil, hemp seed oil, and flax seed oil. The snacks in your diet could comprise of half an avocado flavored with lemon juice or any of the permitted nuts.

Fresh lemon juice, vinegar, mustard, and sea salt are some good choices for your condiments and seasonings. However, you must keep away from any salad dressings or sauces put on sale. Healthy beverages are also required. This can be gotten from green, black or herbal tea or a regular or decaffeinated coffee. To sweeten your tea or coffee, stick with stevia extract. Just Like Sugar is also very much approved as it is a good source of inulin.

Lastly, you must cap it all off with tolerable exercises and by getting the required amount of sleep which is at least eight hours. Ensure that you use only the best quality of foods to make your meals. All vegetables should be totally organic and either fresh or frozen. The best fish to use is the one caught wild. While pastured chicken are also recommended.

One of the great nutritionists who have had so much influence on me advises that it is best to start with your gut all cleaned out and empty. This brings us to component two which involves preparing your gut and removing the bad bugs. To do this, he developed a herbal laxative called Swiss Kriss. This laxative can be found in any pharmacy. Using it, however, is optional. It should be taken the night before the three-day cleanse. Component three takes it a step further by providing support from supplements. The recommended supplements include Oregon grape root extract or its active ingredient, Berberine, grapefruit seed extract, mushrooms, and spices like black pepper and cinnamon which eliminate fungi and parasites.

Returning to your old eating ways after the three day fast is destroying all that has been built. This will permit the previously evicted bad bugs to return for their pound of flesh. The end of the three day fast will see that good bugs replace the bad ones in your gut, you will have lost up to four pounds, and there will be a drastic alleviation of chances of inflammation.

However, your efforts should not end here. Immediately move to phase two. The three day fast will not be a walk in the park. You must be determined to make it to the end because your body will crave for all the harmful foods which you previously consumed. You may also get very hungry and lack some energy. You can satisfy your hunger with the approved vegetables. Also try drinking lots of clean water. Day 4 after the fast will be the game changer. This is when you move to phase two and begin to regain lost energy. You should move on to phase two on the morning of Day 4.

CHAPTER EIGHT: PHASE 2 - REPAIR AND RESTORE.

Key Takeaways

- *Phase two spans a six week period after which new eating habits are formed.*

- *Foods such as beans and milk are not as healthy as they seem.*

- *Brown bread and brown rice are high in lectin.*

- *Undercooked beans is a cause of food poisoning.*

- *Christopher Columbus's discovery of the Americas introduced many high lectin-containing foods.*

In this chapter, I emphasize the ability of your body to self-heal after the harmful foods and anti-healing agents have been dealt with. Phase two begins the following morning after the three-day cleanse. It spans a period of six weeks (minimum) which has repairing and restoring as its goal. The first action in this phase is to put an end to lectin-containing foods that are damaging the walls of your gut. This action begins in the three-day cleanse and continues in phase two.

Remember that it is the things you stop eating that make more impact on your body. Hence you must discard foods that help the bad bacteria in your gut survive. You have seen many of these foods as healthy before however they are actually killers. In the course of the first two weeks, you will already begin to experience significant changes. These changes may come with loss of energy, muscle cramps as well as headaches. However, at the end of the six-week period, new and healthy habits would have been established.

I have divided the foods in your diet for the first two weeks into foods you can eat and those you should abstain from. If you respond well after the first two weeks, you can gradually begin to add some lectin-containing foods to your diet. However, it is advisable to stay the course for the complete six weeks before doing this. As you begin to follow strictly the foods on this diet, have it in mind that you must not refer back to your old eating habits.

In the list of approved foods we have oils which include algae oil, olive oil, coconut oil, MCT oil, avocado oil, macadamia oil. Erythritol and xylitol are good sources for your sweeteners. For your nuts and seeds, go for macadamia nuts, hazelnuts, chestnuts, pine nuts. All kinds of vinegars devoid of sugar are permitted. Do not use chili pepper for your seasoning, cinnamon is a better choice. In making your ice-cream, use stevia, Just Like Sugar, inulin. Use the best quality of broccoli, Brussels sprouts, cauliflower, Bok choy, Napa cabbage for your vegetables.

Pasta Slim, Kelp noodles, Miracle noodles, Miracle rice and Korean sweet potato noodles are on the list of acceptable noodles. For dairy products, acceptable foods include Real Parmesan, French/Italian butter, Buffalo butter; for fruits, avocados, blueberries, raspberries, strawberries, blackberries, cherries. Bison, venison, boar, elk, lamb, beef are good sources for your meat. Find resistant starches in bread and bagels made by Barely Bread and Julian Bakery Paleo Wraps. Chicken, turkey, ostrich, duck or goose for your source of poultry must be pastured.

The foods that you are not allowed to consume include refined starchy foods such as pasta, rice potato, milk, bread, crackers, cookies, cereal, and sugar. Vegetables such as peas, green beans, tofu, soy edamame. Nuts and seeds such as pumpkin, sunflower, chia peanuts. Fruits such as cucumbers, zucchini, pumpkins, any kind of squashes. Oils such as soy, grape seed, corn, safflower. Our ancestors never ate any of these foods because they only began to be cultivated just ten thousand years ago. The goal of this list is not to eliminate all the lectins in your diet rather it is to help you put a check your intake of it.

Lectins thrive in form of Wheat Germ Agglutinin (WGA) in the bran bread which makes the bread brown. It is also present in the hull of rice. This is why several efforts have been put in by your ancestors to get rid of the bran and the hull which will produce white bread and white rice respectively. Beans, peas, soybeans of the legume family are the highest lectin-containing foods. Undercooked beans for food poisoning while canned beans can raise your blood pressure.

This is therefore ironical to the idea that they are health foods. Milk gotten from cows specifically, which is also seen as a good source of healthy food, is actually not as healthy as we perceive it to be. The lectin-like casein A-1 protein in it can be harmful to the body. The only safe milk comes from goats and sheep. Their milk, in spite of containing cancer causing Neu5Gc, is approved on the Plant Paradox Program.

Most of the plants with harmful and deadly lectins today came about with Christopher Columbus's discovery of the Americas. Among these is the peanut which is actually a legume and not a nut. With high lectin content, it is one of the causes of cancer. The cashew nut also surprises everyone in turning out not to be a nut. They are agents of inflammation and rashes being in the same botanical family as poison ivy. Corn and quinoa are grains high in lectin which originated in America. The harmful effects of corn were so bad that it was banned in France in 1900 and allowed for use only in fattening pigs. The squash family, exclusive of the cucumber, are also very high in lectin. So are the oils that I did not list as part of the approved foods. An example of this is canola oil.

In phase two of the program, you must be willing to make the sacrifice of running the full six weeks course. After the first two weeks, you would have very encouraging results but that doesn't mean that you have successfully eliminated all of the bad bacteria in your gut. Some of them may still be hanging around and planning their comeback. This is why you must complete the six weeks to flush them entirely out. In the period of this six weeks, continue to abstain from the foods on the list of harmful lectin-containing foods.

As you do this, strictly adhere to the list of approved foods such as resistant starches, inulin, mushrooms, vegetables, lemon juice and vinegars, figs and dates. For patients who are diagnosed with IBS, crucifers such as sauerkraut under the cabbage family should be overcooked before eaten. You are also advised to do away with the use of antibiotics if possible. You are permitted to use antacids such as Rolaids or Tums. Tylenol should also take the place of your use of NSAIDs.

CHAPTER NINE: PHASE 3 - REAP THE REWARDS

Key Takeaways

- *Beans are a good source of resistant starch.*

- *Protein from beans guarantees longevity more than animal protein.*

- *White basmati rice from India is the best kind of rice to re-introduce into your diet.*

- *Fish and shellfish are better choices for non-vegans over red meat.*

- *Sorghum and millet are the grains with the least amount of lectins.*

Phase three is where you are rewarded for all your efforts. As far as you have faithfully followed the Plant Paradox Program, you will regain your desired weight. But first, you must understand that the program is not just a quick-fix diet. It must become a part and parcel of you.

By doing this, you will find out if your gut bugs are strong enough to support your body and also if you can bring back some lectins into your diet. One of the signs that show that you can start introducing lectins into your gut is that your stools are pushed out in a way that you do not need toilet paper. Other signs include an end to hurting joints, brain fog, acne, and insomnia.

An end to the above mentioned problems is a signal that you can move on to phase three. Phase three exposes you to the fact that the program should really become a part of you. Once it becomes a part of you, you are on your way to living long and living a healthy life. You must continue to adhere strictly to the list of approved foods especially the ones that are grown locally. When the good bugs are back in your system, you must include ketogenic fats such as MCT oil or coconut oil in your diet.

As we've said earlier, going back to your old eating habits or eating the foods that are not approved will invite the bad bugs back into your gut. However, when your good bugs are strong enough to support and protect your system, you can introduce heirloom tomatoes and peppers (without seeds) into your diet, as well as little amounts of legumes. Protein from animals should be restricted to nothing more than 2 ounces daily. Also keep on consuming the recommended of phase two.

The truth is that you cannot do without beans and other legumes forever. In an attempt to run tests on your gut capacity, you can bring back legumes into your diet by cooking them in a pressure cooker. Beans provides your gut bugs with useful resistant starches. The protein gotten from beans guarantees living into a ripe old age more than the protein gotten from animals.

If you're introducing rice back into your diet, it is safe to stick with white basmati rice from India. This is because it does not contain Wheat Germ Agglutinin (WGA) which causes heart disease. Indian white basmati rice is very high on resistant starch. This starch becomes even more resistant when the cooked rice is refrigerated afterwards and is warmed up before use. However, sorghum and millet still remain the best grains with the least amount of lectins.

The harmful effects of animal protein are highlighted the more as we see that meat contributes to obesity just like sugar does. It is therefore safe to stick to fish or shellfish which have no such effect. It is unlike red meat which causes cancer and heart disease with its Neu5Gc content. Studies have also shown that Seventh-day Adventists who are vegans tend to live the longest. This shows that avoiding protein from animals lead to longer life among people.

CHAPTER 10: THE KETO PLANT PARADOX INTENSIVE CARE PROGRAM

Key Takeaways

- *Lectins and LPSs are the cause of many health conditions.*

- *Mitochondria converts sugars and fats into energy.*

- *Sugar is sent to your mitochondria via insulin secreted by your pancreas*

- *Ketones in plant fats are useful to you.*

- *Animal proteins, fruits and sugars are number one enemy.*

- *Fat is good for your body.*

If there's one message that I have been stressing ever since, it is that we must put an end to the harmful effects of lectins in the body. Lectins are responsible for the destruction of the intestinal barrier. This results in many cases ranging from diabetes to cancer to Alzheimer's disease. The presence of lectins in the body makes the glial cells surround and protect the nerve from any incoming substance. This leads to the blocking off of nutrients from food and the eventual death of the nerves. With the presence of lectins and lipopolysaccharides (LPSs), sugars and fats are acted upon by mitochondria. Mitochondria releases ATP which is the molecule responsible for producing energy.

Before now, the mitochondria converted consumed sugar and protein into ATP during daytime. Because there is no incoming sugar or protein at night, the mitochondria's job becomes to burn slowly a type of fat called ketones. Mitochondria acts on these ketones to create ATP at night. The mitochondria's job also continues through summer and winter when incoming food is plentiful and when it is not. However, it could work too much and get exhausted. In this case, your brain becomes starved and cancer cells begin to troop in to utilize the unused sugar lying around in waste.

Your pancreas normally has the job of secreting insulin to send this sugar to your mitochondria. Insulin is rejected if the mitochondria cannot accept it. However, your pancreas does not get aware of this as it continues to secrete more insulin for your mitochondria. This is known as insulin resistance.

In light of this, the safest advice would be to reduce your intake of sugar and protein. Hence, your mitochondria will be focused on burning all the stored fat in the body as fuel. However, this cannot happen if your stored body fat is not converted into ketone by an enzyme called lipase. Ketone is a kind of fat that the body can use. With the consumption of the American diet, comes a lot of insulin and this places difficulty on the production of ketones from body fat.

This is where plants come through with a miracle. Ketones are found in plant fats and this can be of use to you. As we've said earlier, your mitochondria uses these ketones to create ATP. However, this is impossible for cancer patients as cancer cells require huge amounts of sugar and fructose for their growth. This is unlike normal cells do. What this educates us to do is to starve ourselves and especially every cancer patient of these sugars and fruits.

Diabetic patients get to have their ketones sent straight to their mitochondria without the aid of insulin. What we should therefore point out as the enemy is protein, carbs and fruit. Diabetes is caused by too much of these for the mitochondria to handle. Like we have also pointed out in previous chapters, fruit is toxic to your body. Kidney failure is caused mainly by fructose when it is converted to triglycerides. In the Keto Plant Paradox Intensive Program, you will have the ultimate goal of clearing out the lectins, fruits and animal protein that are bad news for your kidneys.

A disorder in your mitochondria is responsible for any health condition you have. If you're a patient suffering from a health condition, I recommend that you strictly follow the Keto Plant Paradox Intensive Care Program List of Acceptable Foods. This list is totally against animal proteins, fruits or seeded vegetables. In the list of these acceptable foods, olive oil, coconut oil, macadamia oil, avocado oil, red palm oil pass for the approved kinds of oil. For flours: coconut, almond, hazelnut, chestnut will do. For sweeteners: it will be stevia, Just Like Sugar, inulin, monk fruit. Your ice-cream can be from coconut and all kinds of olives are permitted. Macadamia nuts are the recommended kind of nuts and seeds.

For your dairy products: French/Italian butter, buffalo butter, ghee, goat butter, goat cheese, sheep cheese, coconut yogurt are great choices. Broccoli, Brussels sprouts, cauliflower, bok choy, Napa cabbage, Chinese cabbage, arugula, watercress and well as radicchio are also great choices of vegetables. Your wine should consist of strictly 6 oz. of red wine per day. For fish: whitefish, freshwater bass, canned tuna, Hawaiian fish, shrimp, crab, lobster, scallops and oysters can do the job. Bison, wild game, venison, and boar can be on the menu for your meat.

The Keto Plant Paradox Intensive Care Program should be followed for the rest of your life if you have cancer or neurological issues. You may stay on the program for two to three months if your health condition is obesity, diabetes, or kidney failure. I must remind you here again that this program should not be considered as a quick-fix. It is something that becomes a part of your life.

CHAPTER 11: PLANT PARADOX SUPPLEMENT RECOMMENDATIONS

Key Takeaways

- *Phytochemicals in plants and animals provide us with a nutritious diet.*

- *A mutation in the MTHFR genes causes inability to create the active forms of Methylfolate and Methylcobalamin.*

- *Polyphenols help in dilating your blood vessels.*

- *The phytochemicals in greens make you less of a sugar lover.*

- *Bad bacteria cannot consume psyllium husks.*

- *Omega-3 fats boosts your memory.*

The Plant Paradox Program consists of a wide array of nutrient supplements. This is because fruits, vegetables and grains do not provide us with the nutrients we really need. Our ancestral diet consisted of over 250 different plants. Plants were the source of their nutritious diet. As at the time when they lived, the organic loam soil was extremely rich in bacteria and fungi. These contributed to phytochemicals in the plants and animals that our ancestors consumed. Today, however, staying true to an organic diet such as the 250 different plants does not guarantee that you get all your required nutrients. This brings in the place of supplements which provide you with your much needed nutrients.

There are several supplements which many people are in dire need of. One of them is Vitamin D3. Many of my patients have tested to be Vitamin D3 deficient. They therefore need a large amount of supplements to bounce back to what is normal. 5000 IUs of Vitamin D3 daily is recommended for replacement when you're just starting out on the program. Patients with autoimmune diseases should begin with 10,000 IUs a day.

The B vitamins are another important set of supplements. They include Methylfolate and Methylcobalamin which are both produced by gut bacteria. A great number of the world's population experience difficulty in making the active form of these two vitamins due to a mutation in the methylenetetrahydrofolate reductase (MTHFR) genes. The cure to this condition is a daily dose of a methylfolate 1000 mcg tablet or a 1000 to 5000 mcg methyl B12 placed beneath your tongue. B vitamin supplements send a methyl group to an amino acid called homocysteine in your system. This makes the homocysteine harmless and helps the supplement bring down high cholesterol levels.

Moving on, I also highlight six must-have supplements for everyone which I termed as the G6. They include polyphenols, green plant phytochemicals, prebiotics, lectin blockers, sugar defense and long chain omega-3s. Polyphenols top the list of important compounds missing in many people's diet. They are designed by plants and are beneficial in actively dilating your blood vessels. I recommend a dosage of polyphenols in supplement form of 100 mg of both grape seed extract and resveratrol, and 25 to 100 mg of pine tree bark extract daily.

Green plant phytochemicals will reinforce the amount of greens in your system. This will be needed because your cravings for greens will be on the rise when you are on the Plant Paradox Program. The phytochemicals in greens turn your focus away from sugars which are bad news for us. Two tablets of 500 mg spinach extract capsules daily will be of great help to you.

The bugs that live on you and within you are termed probiotics while prebiotics are the compounds on the menu for probiotics to eat. Many of this compounds such as psyllium powder or husks work effectively in cases of constipation. These psyllium husks can be eaten by the good bugs in your gut but not by the bad bugs. GundryMD PrebioThrive is a supplement I designed to give you the same value that the prebiotics found in nine cups of vegetables daily would.

In the case of mistakenly eating lectin-containing foods, you do not need to fret. There are numerous lectin-absorbing compounds available to address the issue. One of them is my designed formula called GundryMD Lectin Shield. I advise that you take two capsules of it before a meal you suspect to have a high lectin content. A 500 mg dosage of D-mannose twice daily is also very helpful especially for patients with urinary tract infections.

Consumption of sugar in simple carbohydrates and fructose in fruits and corn syrup is something we are all guilty of. I developed a supplement called GundryMD Glucose Defense which creates changes in the effects of sugars on your body and insulin. This supplement is a mixture of chromium, zinc, selenium, cinnamon bark extract, berberine, turmeric extract, and black pepper extract. CinSulin from Costco is also a wonderful supplement in this regard. It is a combination of chromium and cinnamon. Two capsules of it daily along with 30 mg of zinc once a day, 150 mcg of selenium daily, 250 mg of berberine twice daily, and 200 mg of turmeric extract twice daily.

Long-chain omega-3s are another set of highly important supplements for people deficient in the omega-3 fatty acids EPA (eicosapentaenoic acid) and DHA (docosahexaenoic acid). Studies have proven that high levels of omega-3 fats in the blood leads to a more efficient memory. I recommend you take fish oils of sardines and anchovies. Your dosage should be 1000 mg of DHA daily.

These supplements back up your progress made on the Plant Paradox Program. They are not magic wands that will immediately resolve all the harmful sides of the Western diet. One thing they do is to guarantee measurable results and enhance the progress you have made so far.

Made in the USA
Lexington, KY
01 November 2018